- *Comprehensive Workbook*
- *30-Day Guided Journal*

Reality

Transurfing
WORKBOOK

Master the Principles of Vadim Zeland's Reality Transurfing to Manifest Your Desired Life

Attain

Our workbooks and journals are created to support you in practicing and implementing the principles that can transform your life, and enhance your health, wealth, and relationships.

Browse Our Catalog

Belongs to

👤 _____

✉ _____

📞 _____

🐦 _____

📷 _____

♪ _____

Contents

*May the solutions be brought forward to what you came for,
and the knowledge be yours to the questions that are on top on
your tongue.*

*For they are personal and they are unique to you and your path,
and they are ready to be dealt with*

—

indeed, it's a good time for healing.

Preface

elcome to The Reality Transurfing Transformation Workbook, your practical guide to understanding and implementing the groundbreaking concepts of Vadim Zeland's Reality Transurfing.

Reality Transurfing is not just another self-help technique; it's a fundamentally different way of viewing and navigating the world.

Its principles challenge conventional wisdom and open the doors to a reality where you have the power to influence the course of events in your life and manifest your desires.

Creating this workbook was a labor of love and a journey in itself. The teachings of Vadim Zeland have profoundly impacted many lives, and have the potential to transform yours as well.

This workbook is designed to make the complex concepts of Reality Transurfing accessible and practical for anyone who is ready to step into a new, more empowering paradigm of life.

In this workbook, you will find in-depth explanations of the key principles of Reality Transurfing, along with a variety of exercises to help you apply these principles in your daily life.

You will learn to navigate the Space of Variations, overcome pendulums, attract the Wave of Fortune, and much more.

One of the unique features of this workbook is the inclusion of a 30-day guided journal.

This journal is designed to deepen your understanding and experience of Reality Transurfing, offering you space for reflection, self-discovery, and growth.

However, remember that real change requires consistency and practice. The workbook is not meant to be rushed through but to be savored, with time taken to fully engage with the exercises and reflections.

The principles of Reality Transurfing can offer profound changes, but they must be practiced and integrated into your life over time.

Allow this workbook to serve as a valuable tool on your journey of transformation, helping you to tap into the infinite possibilities that exist within the Space of Variations and align with your desired reality.

Here's to manifesting your desired life with Reality Transurfing!

Introduction to Reality Transurfing

Reality Transurfing is a powerful and transformative personal development framework developed by Russian author and quantum physicist Vadim Zeland.

It combines elements of quantum physics, metaphysics, and practical psychology to help individuals shape their reality and create the life they desire.

The main idea behind Reality Transurfing is that our thoughts, beliefs, and energy directly influence the events and circumstances in our lives.

Overview of Reality Transurfing Principles

1. **The Space of Variations:** Also known as the "alternative space" or the "field of information," the Space of Variations is an infinite field containing all possible realities and scenarios.

   Reality Transurfing suggests that we can consciously navigate this field to manifest our desired reality.

2. **Pendulums:** Pendulums are energy structures created by the collective thoughts and beliefs of a group of people. They can exert control over individuals, sapping their energy and directing their actions.

   Learning to identify and free yourself from pendulums is essential in Reality Transurfing.

3. **The Wave of Fortune:** This principle represents a series of positive events and circumstances that come into our lives when we are in alignment with our true selves and our natural life path.

   By maintaining positive thoughts, emotions, and actions, we can attract the Wave of Fortune and experience a continuous flow of favorable situations.

4. **Importance**: Importance is the exaggerated significance we assign to events, people, or objects in our lives. High levels of importance create an imbalance in our energy and attract balancing forces that can hinder our progress.

   Reducing importance is key to manifesting our desired reality.

5. **Balancing Forces:** These are the forces that come into play when there is an imbalance in energy due to excessive importance. Balancing forces can manifest as obstacles, setbacks, or negative events, and their purpose is to restore equilibrium.

   By reducing importance, we can minimize the impact of balancing forces.

6. **Heart and Mind Coordination:** In Reality Transurfing, the heart represents our intuition and true desires, while the mind represents our rational thoughts and beliefs.

   Achieving heart and mind coordination is crucial for manifesting our desired reality, as it ensures that our intentions are aligned with our true selves.

7. **Goals and Doors:** Goals are the desired outcomes we want to achieve, while doors are the unique opportunities and paths that lead to these outcomes.

   Reality Transurfing emphasizes the importance of identifying our true goals and finding the doors that are most suited to our individual strengths and passions.

End of Chapter Exercises

Reflect on your initial understanding of Reality Transurfing principles.

How do they resonate with your current worldview?

What principle intrigues you the most, and why?

Notes

Pendulums

Pendulums are energy structures created by the collective thoughts, beliefs, and emotions of a group of people.

These structures can be both positive and negative, depending on the nature of the energy they emit.

Pendulums can exert control over individuals by feeding on their energy and directing their actions.

Identifying and freeing yourself from the influence of pendulums is crucial in Reality Transurfing, as it allows you to regain control over your own energy and destiny.

Identifying Pendulums In Your Life

To identify pendulums in your life, consider the following:

1. *Observe your emotions:* Pay attention to situations or interactions that trigger strong emotional reactions in you, such as anger, frustration, or fear.

   These may be signs of a pendulum trying to capture your energy.

2. *Analyze your beliefs*: Reflect on your beliefs and opinions, particularly those that align with popular or widely accepted views. Some of these beliefs may have been influenced by pendulums.

3. *Examine your habits and routines:* Identify activities, habits, or routines that drain your energy and leave you feeling exhausted, unfulfilled, or disconnected from your true self.

   These may be indications of pendulum influence.

4. *Assess your relationships:* Evaluate your relationships and social circles, looking for patterns of codependency, manipulation, or unhealthy dynamics.

   These can be signs of pendulum-driven connections.

Exercises to Free Yourself from Pendulums

1. *Awareness:* The first step in freeing yourself from pendulums is becoming aware of their presence and influence in your life.

   Regularly practice self-reflection and self-observation to identify the pendulums you're interacting with.

2. *Emotional detachment:* When you notice yourself getting emotionally triggered by a pendulum, practice detaching from the situation by taking a few deep breaths and reminding yourself that your energy is valuable and should not be wasted on external influences.

3. *Change your focus:* Redirect your attention and energy away from the pendulum and towards activities that align with your true desires and goals.

   This can help you weaken the pendulum's hold over you and regain control over your own energy.

4. *Create a protective shield:* Visualize a protective energy shield surrounding you, blocking any negative influences or energy-draining forces.

   This mental imagery can help strengthen your resolve to stay unaffected by pendulums.

5. *Set boundaries:* Establish clear boundaries with people or situations that are connected to pendulums, limiting your exposure and interaction with them.

6. *Cultivate positive energy:* Focus on building a positive, supportive environment for yourself, filled with activities, people, and experiences that uplift and energize you.

   This will make it more difficult for pendulums to influence you and drain your energy.

End of Chapter Exercises

Consider your life and identify some potential pendulums that could be influencing your decisions and actions.

How do they affect your daily life and behavior?

What steps can you take to reduce their impact?

The Space of Variations

The Space of Variations, also known as the "alternative space" or the "field of information," is a concept in Reality Transurfing that represents an infinite field containing all possible realities, scenarios, and potential outcomes.

It is a realm of endless possibilities, where every conceivable event or situation exists simultaneously.

By understanding and consciously navigating the Space of Variations, you can manifest your desired reality and create the life you truly want.

Exploring the Space of Variations

To explore the Space of Variations, you need to develop a heightened sense of awareness and an open-minded attitude.

Embrace the idea that there are countless potential realities available to you, and that your current experience is just one of many possible scenarios.

As you become more familiar with this concept, you'll be better equipped to navigate the Space of Variations and attract the reality you desire.

Techniques for Navigating the Space of Variations

1. **Visualization:** One of the most powerful tools for navigating the Space of Variations is visualization.

   By regularly envisioning your desired reality in vivid detail, you can align yourself with that specific variation and increase the likelihood of manifesting it in your life.

2. **Intention setting:** Set clear intentions for the reality you want to experience.

   Be specific and focused, as this will help you to direct your energy and attention towards the desired variation in the space of possibilities.

3. **Emotional resonance:** Cultivate the emotions and feelings that correspond to your desired reality.

   By doing so, you create an energetic resonance that attracts the corresponding variation from the Space of Variations.

4. **Action and persistence:** Take consistent action towards your goals and desires.

   This helps you to navigate through the Space of Variations and move closer to your intended reality.

5. **Mindfulness and present moment awareness:** Practice being fully present in the moment and observe your thoughts, feelings, and actions without judgment.

   This heightened awareness will help you identify when you're drifting away from your desired reality and make conscious adjustments to realign with your goals.

6. **Heart and mind coordination:** Achieve unity between your heart and mind, ensuring that your desires and intentions are aligned with your true self.

   This harmony is essential for effectively navigating the Space of Variations and manifesting your desired reality.

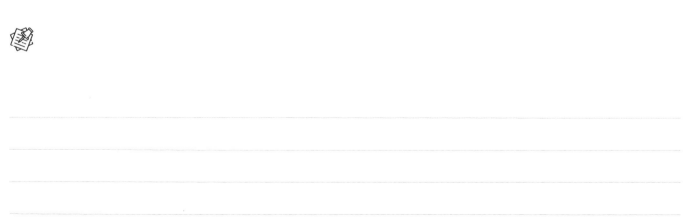

28

End of Chapter Exercises

Imagine the infinite possibilities that exist within the Space of Variations.

What variations appeal to you the most?

How would your life look if you navigated towards your desired variations?

The Wave of Fortune

The Wave of Fortune is a concept in Reality Transurfing that represents a series of positive events and circumstances that come into our lives when we are in alignment with our true selves and our natural life path.

When we ride the Wave of Fortune, we experience a continuous flow of favorable situations, opportunities, and synchronicities that help us manifest our desired reality.

There is a tide in the affairs of men
Which, taken at the flood, leads on to fortune;
Omitted, all the voyage of their life
Is bound in shallows and in miseries.
On such a full sea are we now afloat;
And we must take the current when it serves,
Or lose our ventures."

— William Shakespeare , Julius Caesar

Understanding the Wave of Fortune

The Wave of Fortune is not something that occurs by chance or luck; rather, it is a state that we can consciously attract by maintaining positive thoughts, emotions, and actions.

When we are aligned with our true desires and intentions, we create an energetic resonance that attracts positive experiences and opportunities from the Space of Variations.

Exercises for Attracting the Wave of Fortune

1. **Cultivate gratitude:** Regularly practice gratitude by focusing on the positive aspects of your life and expressing appreciation for what you have.

   This positive energy helps to align you with the Wave of Fortune.

2. **Maintain a positive attitude:** Cultivate an optimistic and positive attitude, even in challenging situations.

   This mindset helps you to stay in alignment with the Wave of Fortune and attract more positive experiences.

3. **Visualize success:** Spend time each day visualizing your desired reality and the positive experiences you want to attract.

   This mental rehearsal helps to align your energy with the Wave of Fortune.

4. **Set clear intentions:** Define your goals and intentions, focusing on what you want to achieve and the positive experiences you want to create.

   By setting clear intentions, you can better align yourself with the Wave of Fortune.

5. **Take inspired action:** Act on your intuition and follow your heart, pursuing the opportunities and paths that resonate with your true self.

   This inspired action will help you ride the Wave of Fortune and manifest your desired reality.

6. **Surround yourself with positive influences:** Create a supportive environment filled with positive people, experiences, and resources that inspire and uplift you.

   This positive energy will help you stay in alignment with the Wave of Fortune.

7. **Practice self-care:** Prioritize your physical, emotional, and mental well-being by engaging in regular self-care activities.

   This will help you maintain a balanced and positive state, which is essential for attracting the Wave of Fortune.

End of Chapter Exercises

Reflect on a time when you experienced a streak of good luck or a flow of positive events.

Can you associate it with a particular mindset or actions?

How can you attract the Wave of Fortune more frequently?

Importance and Balancing Forces

In Reality Transurfing, importance plays a critical role in shaping our reality and attracting balancing forces.

Importance refers to the exaggerated significance we assign to events, people, or objects in our lives.

When we attribute excessive importance to something, we create an energetic imbalance that invites balancing forces to restore equilibrium.

Balancing forces can manifest as obstacles, setbacks, or negative events, which can hinder our progress and prevent us from manifesting our desired reality.

The Role of Importance in Reality Transurfing

High levels of importance can create several issues:

1. *Distorted perception:* Excessive importance can distort our perception of reality, leading to irrational fears, unrealistic expectations, and self-imposed limitations.

2. *Energy imbalance:* When we attach too much importance to something, we create an imbalance in our energy, making it difficult to attract and maintain positive experiences and opportunities.

3. *Attracting balancing forces:* The energetic imbalance caused by excessive importance invites balancing forces to intervene, often manifesting as challenges, obstacles, or negative events in our lives.

By recognizing the role of importance in Reality Transurfing, we can take conscious steps to reduce its impact on our lives and minimize the influence of balancing forces.

Techniques for Reducing Importance and Balancing Forces

1. *Awareness and observation:* Practice self-awareness and observe your thoughts and emotions, especially when you notice feelings of anxiety, fear, or attachment.

   Recognize the importance you may be assigning to a situation or object and consciously choose to let go of it.

2. *Reframe your perspective:* Shift your perspective to see situations, people, or objects as less significant or crucial to your overall happiness and well-being.

   This can help reduce the importance you place on them and restore energetic balance.

3. *Focus on the process, not the outcome:* Instead of fixating on a specific outcome or result, focus on the actions you can take and the effort you put in.

   By concentrating on the process, you can reduce the importance of the outcome and minimize the impact of balancing forces.

4. *Practice detachment:* Cultivate an attitude of detachment, allowing events to unfold naturally without trying to control or force them.

   This can help you release the importance you place on specific outcomes and remain open to a wider range of possibilities.

5. *Develop self-confidence:* Strengthen your self-confidence and belief in your abilities, knowing that you can handle any situation, regardless of the outcome.

   This can help you reduce the importance you place on external factors and focus on your own growth and development.

6. *Embrace uncertainty:* Accept that life is inherently uncertain and that unexpected events or changes can occur at any time.

   This mindset can help you release excessive importance and be more adaptable and resilient in the face of challenges.

By implementing these techniques, you can reduce the importance you place on various aspects of your life and minimize the influence of balancing forces.

This will help you maintain a more balanced and harmonious energy, allowing you to effectively navigate the Space of Variations and manifest your desired reality.

End of Chapter Exercises

Consider a situation where you attached excessive importance and it resulted in balancing forces acting against you.

How did the situation unfold?

How can you manage importance in future situations to avoid attracting balancing forces?

The Heart and Mind Coordination

In Reality Transurfing, heart and mind coordination is a crucial aspect of manifesting your desired reality.

The heart represents your intuition, true desires, and inner wisdom, while the mind represents your rational thoughts, beliefs, and decision-making processes.

Achieving unity between the heart and mind ensures that your intentions, actions, and energy are aligned with your true self, allowing you to effectively navigate the Space of Variations and attract your desired reality.

Understanding Heart and Mind Coordination

When your heart and mind are in harmony, you experience a sense of inner peace, clarity, and purpose.

This alignment allows you to make decisions and take actions that are congruent with your true desires and goals.

On the other hand, when the heart and mind are in conflict, you may experience confusion, self-doubt, and inner turmoil, making it difficult to manifest your desired reality.

Exercises to Achieve Heart and Mind Unity

1. **Self-reflection:** Regularly engage in self-reflection to gain a deeper understanding of your true desires, values, and beliefs.

   This will help you identify any misalignments between your heart and mind and make necessary adjustments.

2. **Meditation:** Practice meditation to quiet your mind and connect with your inner wisdom.

   This can help you tune into your heart's guidance and achieve greater heart and mind coordination.

3. **Journaling:** Write about your thoughts, feelings, and desires in a journal.

   This can help you gain clarity on what truly matters to you and identify any discrepancies between your heart and mind.

4. **Mindfulness:** Cultivate present-moment awareness by observing your thoughts, emotions, and actions without judgment.

   This can help you recognize when your heart and mind are in conflict and make conscious adjustments to realign them.

5. **Intuition development:** Practice listening to and trusting your intuition, allowing it to guide you in making decisions and taking actions that align with your true self.

6. **Emotional healing:** Address any unresolved emotions or past traumas that may be causing internal conflict between your heart and mind.

7. **Affirmations**: Use positive affirmations to reinforce the unity between your heart and mind. For example, repeat phrases like

   "*I am in harmony with my true self*" or

   "*My heart and mind are aligned with my highest good.*"

By practicing these exercises, you can achieve greater heart and mind coordination, which is essential for effectively navigating the Space of Variations and manifesting the life you desire.

Notes

End of Chapter Exercises

Reflect on a decision you made that was *in harmony with both your heart and mind.*

How did it feel?

How can you work towards achieving this heart and mind unity more often?

Goals and Doors

In Reality Transurfing, goals and doors represent the desired outcomes you wish to achieve and the unique paths or opportunities that lead to those outcomes.

Identifying your true goals and finding your own doors are essential steps in creating a reality that aligns with your heart's desires and intentions.

Identifying Your True Goals

To identify your true goals, consider the following:

1. **Reflect on your values:** Determine what is truly important to you, and base your goals on your core values and beliefs.

    This will ensure that your goals are authentic and aligned with your true self.

2. **Follow your passion:** Identify activities, interests, or pursuits that genuinely excite and inspire you.

    Your true goals should be connected to your passions and reflect what you truly love to do.

3. **Assess your strengths and talents:** Consider your natural abilities and strengths, and choose goals that leverage these gifts.

    By focusing on what you're good at, you'll be more likely to succeed and enjoy the journey.

4. **Visualize your ideal life:** Envision the life you genuinely desire, without limitations or expectations from others.

    This will help you clarify your true goals and prioritize what really matters.

Techniques for Finding and Opening Your Own Doors

1. **Stay open to possibilities:** Embrace the idea that there are countless opportunities and paths available to you.

   Be open to exploring new ideas, experiences, and perspectives that can lead you to your own doors.

2. **Cultivate self-awareness:** Regularly practice self-reflection and self-observation to better understand your desires, strengths, and motivations.

   This heightened awareness can help you recognize the doors that are aligned with your true goals.

3. **Trust your intuition:** Listen to your inner guidance and trust your instincts when evaluating potential doors or opportunities.

   Your intuition can often help you identify the best path forward.

4. **Take action:** Don't be afraid to take risks and pursue opportunities that resonate with your true goals.

   By taking action, you can open doors and create new possibilities for yourself.

5. **Develop resilience:** Understand that setbacks and obstacles are a natural part of the journey towards your goals.

   Cultivate resilience and determination to overcome challenges and continue moving forward.

6. **Network and connect:** Build relationships with others who share your interests, passions, and goals.

   Networking can lead to new doors and opportunities that you may not have discovered on your own.

7. **Stay flexible and adaptable:** Be willing to adjust your plans and strategies as you gain new insights or encounter unexpected circumstances.

   Staying flexible and adaptable can help you navigate the ever-changing landscape of opportunities and find the doors that are most aligned with your true goals.

By identifying your true goals and using these techniques to find and open your own doors, you can create a reality that reflects your authentic desires and intentions, and successfully manifest the life you truly want to live.

Notes

End of Chapter Exercises

What are your true goals in life?
Are they imposed by society or truly yours?

Consider the doors that may open when you pursue these true goals.

What steps can you take to find and open these doors?

Meditation Techniques in Reality Transurfing

In Vadim Zeland's groundbreaking work, "Reality Transurfing", the principles aren't just theoretical concepts; they are practical tools designed to guide us in shaping our reality.

While the techniques outlined may not strictly fall under traditional meditation practices, they carry a similar essence.

They encourage a profound state of mindfulness, presence, and self-awareness, functioning as powerful psychological exercises that catalyze transformation.

The Slides Technique

Imagine holding a small rectangular piece of film, a slide, in your hands.

On this slide is a scene that encapsulates your desired reality— every detail, color, and emotion is captured vividly.

Now, imagine projecting this slide onto your current reality, immersing yourself entirely in this image.

This is the essence of the Slides technique.

Constructing a slide requires creativity and deep thought, the ability to dream vividly, and see every nuance of your desired reality.

The slide isn't merely a vision but a holistic sensory experience— feel the emotions, hear the sounds, and engage with this reality in your mind's eye.

The more you project this slide, the more your current reality begins to morph to reflect your desired one.

Outer Intention Visualization

Reality Transurfing posits that there are two types of intentions: inner intention, the will of the individual, and outer intention, the will of the universe.

Outer intention visualization involves seeing the process that leads to your goal.

It's not about fantasizing the end result, but rather visualizing each step you take towards your goal.

This technique aligns you with the universe's flow, creating a path of least resistance towards your desired outcome.

Coordination of Intention

This technique seeks to create harmony between your heart and mind, an essential aspect of Reality Transurfing.

When your heart's desires and your mind's logic align, they create a powerful force for manifesting your reality.

This alignment is not about compromise but about unity, a shared vision between heart and mind.

It's a dance, a beautiful interaction where each entity respects and supports the other.

Pendulum Defeating Technique

Pendulums, as Zeland describes, are energy structures that feed on our attention and can sway our actions.

Recognizing these pendulums is the first step.

Then, through conscious choice, we refuse to give them our energy.

This is not about conflict but about non-engagement.

We acknowledge the pendulum's presence but choose not to dance to its tune.

Instead, we direct our energy towards the reality we desire.

The Void Technique

Finally, we have the Void Technique.

Picture being in an open, infinite space– a void.

In this space, you're free from pendulums, societal pressures, and any other influence that strays you from your path.

This void is a state of pure potentiality, where you're detached from distractions, enabling you to select your path without external influences.

30-Day Guided Journal

Week 1:
Understanding Reality Transurfing

Notes

Day.**01**

Introduction to Reality Transurfing

Book Insight

Reality Transurfing helps you navigate the infinite possibilities in the Space of Variations to create your desired reality

Daily Challenge

Identify one area of your life where you'd like to apply Reality Transurfing principles and set a specific intention for change.

Affirmation

I am the conscious creator of my reality.

Write down your understanding of Reality Transurfing in your own words.

List three areas of your life where you'd like to apply Reality Transurfing principles.

Notes

Day.02
Pendulums

Book Insight

Pendulums are energy structures that can influence our thoughts, emotions, and actions, often draining our energy.

Daily Challenge

Observe your interactions throughout the day and identify any pendulums that may be influencing you.

Affirmation

I am free from the influence of pendulums and in control of my own energy.

Reflect on the pendulums present in your life.

List at least three pendulums that you feel have a strong influence on you.

Choose one pendulum and write about the steps you can take to reduce its influence on your life.

Notes

Day.**03**
The Space of Variations

Book Insight

The Space of Variations is an infinite field of possibilities where all realities exist simultaneously.

Daily Challenge

Spend 10 minutes visualizing your desired reality and pay attention to the emotions and insights that arise.

Affirmation

I consciously navigate the Space of Variations to manifest my desires.

Write about a time when you experienced a shift in reality, whether it was a change in circumstances or a change in perspective.

Describe how you can navigate the Space of Variations more effectively in the future.

Notes

Day.**04**
The Wave of Fortune

Book Insight

The Wave of Fortune is a continuous flow of positive events and opportunities that can be attracted through positive thoughts, emotions, and actions.

Daily Challenge

List three positive actions you can take today to attract the Wave of Fortune.

Affirmation

I am a magnet for the Wave of Fortune and attract abundance in all areas of my life.

List three recent events or experiences that you feel were part of your Wave of Fortune.

Write about the steps you can take to attract and maintain the Wave of Fortune in your life.

Notes

Day.**05**

Importance and Balancing Forces

Book Insight

Importance creates imbalance in our lives and can attract balancing forces that hinder our manifestation efforts.

Daily Challenge

Identify a situation where you are placing excessive importance and practice letting go of that importance.

Affirmation

I release the importance I place on events, people, and objects, allowing my reality to unfold with ease.

Reflect on a situation where you placed excessive importance on something and experienced balancing forces as a result.

Write down three techniques you can use to reduce the importance you place on events, people, or objects.

Notes

Day.06
The Heart and Mind Coordination

Book Insight

Aligning your heart and mind leads to greater clarity, intuition, and manifestation power.

Daily Challenge

Practice listening to both your heart and mind when making decisions today.

Affirmation

My heart and mind are in perfect harmony, guiding me towards my true desires.

Describe a decision or situation in which your heart and mind were in conflict.

List three strategies for achieving greater heart and mind coordination.

Notes

Day.**07**
Goals and Doors

Book Insight

Your true goals are aligned with your passions, values, and strengths, and pursuing them opens unique doors and opportunities.

Daily Challenge

Reflect on your true goals and take one actionable step towards achieving them.

Affirmation

I pursue my true goals with passion, courage, and determination.

Write down three true goals that align with your passions, values, and strengths.

Reflect on your current progress towards these goals and identify any doors or opportunities you can pursue to help you achieve them.

Weekly Review and Reflection Template

1. Key Insights and Learnings:

- Reflect on the key insights and learnings from this week's journal entries, activities, and experiences.

- Insight 1:

- Insight 2:

- Insight 3:

2. Application and Progress:

- Consider how you have applied the key insights and learnings in your daily life this week.

- Application 1:

- Application 2:

- Application 3:

- Assess your progress towards your goals and intentions.

- Progress 1:

- Progress 2:

- Progress 3:

3. Challenges and Obstacles:

- Identify any challenges or obstacles you encountered this week and how you overcame them or plan to overcome them.

  - Challenge 1:

  - Challenge 2:

  - Challenge 3:

4. Gratitude and Celebrations:

- List three things you are grateful for this week.

  - Gratitude 1:

  - Gratitude 2:

  - Gratitude 3:

- Celebrate your achievements, successes, and positive experiences from this week.

  - Celebration 1:

  - Celebration 2:

  - Celebration 3:

5. Next Week's Focus:

- Set your intentions and focus for the upcoming week.

    - Intention 1:

    - Intention 2:

    - Intention 3:

- Identify any areas for improvement or adjustments you can make in the coming week.

    - Improvement 1:

    - Improvement 2:

    - Improvement 3:

Take some time to review and complete this template at the end of each week to reflect on your progress, insights, and experiences.

This will help you stay on track with your goals, celebrate your successes, and continually grow and evolve on your Reality Transurfing journey.

Week 2:
Implementing Reality
Transurfing Principles

Notes

Day.08

Practicing Disengagement from Pendulums

Book Insight

Disengaging from pendulums requires awareness, intention, and consistent practice.

Daily Challenge

Practice disengaging from a pendulum you identified last week by redirecting your focus and energy.

Affirmation

I choose to disengage from pendulums that do not serve my highest good.

Reflect on your progress in disengaging from the pendulums you identified last week.

Write about any new pendulums you have noticed and describe how you plan to reduce their influence on your life.

Notes

Day.09

Visualization and the Space of Variations

Book Insight

Visualization is a powerful tool for navigating the Space of Variations and manifesting your desired reality.

Daily Challenge

Spend 15 minutes visualizing your desired reality and pay attention to the emotions and insights that arise.

Affirmation

My vivid visualizations bring my desired reality to life.

Practice visualizing your desired reality for at least 10 minutes.

Write about the experience and any insights or emotions that arose.

Describe how visualization can help you navigate the Space of Variations more effectively.

Notes

Day.10
Gratitude and the Wave of Fortune

Book Insight

Gratitude helps to attract and maintain the Wave of Fortune by focusing on the positive aspects of your life.

Daily Challenge

List five things you are grateful for and reflect on how they contribute to your Wave of Fortune.

Affirmation

I am grateful for the abundance and blessings in my life.

List five things you are grateful for today and reflect on how they contribute to your Wave of Fortune.

Write about how cultivating gratitude can help attract and maintain the Wave of Fortune in your life.

Notes

Day.**11**
Reducing Importance

Book Insight

Reducing importance minimizes the impact of balancing forces and allows your reality to unfold more effortlessly.

Daily Challenge

Practice reducing importance in a situation or goal by reminding yourself of the bigger picture and focusing on the present moment.

Affirmation

I let go of excessive importance, allowing my life to flow with ease and grace.

Choose a situation or goal where you feel you may be placing excessive importance.

Write about how this might be affecting your ability to manifest your desired reality.

Describe the steps you can take to reduce the importance you place on this situation or goal.

Notes

Day.12
Heart and Mind Alignment in Decision-Making

Book Insight

Heart and mind coordination is essential for making decisions that are aligned with your true desires and goals.

Daily Challenge

Practice heart and mind coordination by tuning into your intuition and logic when making decisions today.

Affirmation

My heart and mind work together in harmony, guiding me towards my highest path.

Reflect on a recent decision you made or need to make.

Write about how you can use heart and mind coordination to make the best choice.

Describe any challenges you have faced in achieving heart and mind coordination and how you can overcome them.

Notes

Day.**13**
Taking Action on Your Goals

Book Insight

Taking consistent action towards your true goals helps you manifest your desired reality more effectively.

Daily Challenge

Identify a specific action you can take today to move closer to one of your true goals.

Affirmation

I take inspired action towards my goals with confidence and determination.

Choose one of the true goals you identified last week and write about the specific actions you can take to move closer to achieving it.

Reflect on any obstacles or challenges you may face in pursuing this goal and describe how you can overcome them using Reality Transurfing principles.

Notes

Day.14

Embracing Change and Personal Growth

Book Insight

Embracing change and personal growth supports your Reality Transurfing journey and helps you manifest your desired reality.

Daily Challenge

Reflect on a recent change or personal growth experience and how it has impacted your life.

Affirmation

I embrace change and growth, allowing my reality to evolve in alignment with my true desires.

Write about a recent change or personal growth experience and how it has affected your life.

Reflect on how embracing change and personal growth can support your Reality Transurfing journey.

Weekly Review and Reflection Template

1. Key Insights and Learnings:

- Reflect on the key insights and learnings from this week's journal entries, activities, and experiences.

- Insight 1:

- Insight 2:

- Insight 3:

2. Application and Progress:

- Consider how you have applied the key insights and learnings in your daily life this week.

- Application 1:

- Application 2:

- Application 3:

- Assess your progress towards your goals and intentions.

- Progress 1:

- Progress 2:

- Progress 3:

3. Challenges and Obstacles:

- Identify any challenges or obstacles you encountered this week and how you overcame them or plan to overcome them.

- Challenge 1:

- Challenge 2:

- Challenge 3:

4. Gratitude and Celebrations:

- List three things you are grateful for this week.

- Gratitude 1:

- Gratitude 2:

- Gratitude 3:

- Celebrate your achievements, successes, and positive experiences from this week.

- Celebration 1:

- Celebration 2:

- Celebration 3:

5. Next Week's Focus:

- Set your intentions and focus for the upcoming week.

   - Intention 1:

   - Intention 2:

   - Intention 3:

- Identify any areas for improvement or adjustments you can make in the coming week.

   - Improvement 1:

   - Improvement 2:

   - Improvement 3:

Take some time to review and complete this template at the end of each week to reflect on your progress, insights, and experiences.

This will help you stay on track with your goals, celebrate your successes, and continually grow and evolve on your Reality Transurfing journey.

Week 3:
Deepening Your Reality Transurfing Practice

Day.**15**
Mindfulness and Self-Observation

Book Insight

Mindfulness and self-observation are essential tools for gaining insight into your thoughts, emotions, and actions.

Daily Challenge

Practice mindfulness and self-observation throughout the day, noting any insights or patterns that arise.

Affirmation

I am present and aware, observing my thoughts, emotions, and actions with curiosity and compassion.

Practice mindfulness and self-observation throughout the day.

Write about your experience and any insights you gained about your thoughts, emotions, and actions.

Describe how mindfulness and self-observation can support your Reality Transurfing journey.

Notes

Day.16
Exploring Your Intuition

Book Insight

Strengthening and trusting your intuition supports heart and mind coordination and helps you navigate the Space of Variations more effectively.

Daily Challenge

Spend some time in quiet reflection, tuning into your intuition and noting any guidance or insights that come through.

Affirmation

I trust my intuition to guide me towards my true desires and goals.

Reflect on a recent situation where you followed or ignored your intuition.

Write about the outcome and what you learned from the experience.

Describe how you can strengthen and trust your intuition to support your heart and mind coordination.

Notes

Day.17
Energy Management

Book Insight

Managing your energy effectively helps you maintain your manifestation power and supports your Reality Transurfing journey.

Daily Challenge

Assess your current energy levels and identify any activities or habits that may be draining or boosting your energy.

Affirmation

I conserve and cultivate my energy, using it wisely to create my desired reality.

Assess your current energy levels and identify any factors that may be draining or boosting your energy.

Write about the steps you can take to conserve and increase your energy to support your Reality Transurfing practice.

Notes

Day.18

Reframing Challenges and Setbacks

Book Insight

Reframing challenges and setbacks using Reality Transurfing principles helps you maintain a positive mindset and attract the Wave of Fortune.

Daily Challenge

Reflect on a recent challenge or setback and practice reframing it using Reality Transurfing principles.

Affirmation

I see challenges as opportunities for growth and transformation, bringing me closer to my desired reality.

Reflect on a recent challenge or setback and write about how you can reframe it using Reality Transurfing principles.

Describe how this reframing can help you maintain a positive mindset and attract the Wave of Fortune.

Day.19

Letting Go of Expectations

Book Insight

Letting go of expectations allows you to create a more authentic and aligned reality.

Daily Challenge

Identify an area of your life where you may be holding onto expectations and practice letting go of them.

Affirmation

I release expectations and trust the unfolding of my unique path.

Identify an area of your life where you may be holding onto expectations, either from yourself or others.

Write about how you can release these expectations and create a more authentic and aligned reality.

Notes

Day.20
Embracing Synchronicities

Book Insight

Embracing synchronicities supports your Reality Transurfing journey by guiding you towards your desired reality.

Daily Challenge

Pay attention to any synchronicities or meaningful coincidences that occur today and reflect on their significance.

Affirmation

I am open to recognizing and following synchronicities on my path.

Reflect on any recent synchronicities or meaningful coincidences you have experienced.

Write about how you can be more open to recognizing and embracing synchronicities to support your Reality Transurfing journey.

Notes

Day.21
Continuous Learning and Growth

Book Insight

Continuous learning and growth are essential for deepening your understanding of Reality Transurfing and manifesting your desired reality.

Daily Challenge

Identify a book, course, or resource related to Reality Transurfing or personal growth that you would like to explore.

Affirmation

I am committed to continuous learning and growth on my Reality Transurfing journey.

Identify a book, course, or resource related to Reality Transurfing or personal growth that you would like to explore.

Write about how you can commit to continuous learning and growth on your Reality Transurfing journey.

Weekly Review and Reflection Template

1. Key Insights and Learnings:

- Reflect on the key insights and learnings from this week's journal entries, activities, and experiences.

    - Insight 1:

    - Insight 2:

    - Insight 3:

2. Application and Progress:

- Consider how you have applied the key insights and learnings in your daily life this week.

    - Application 1:

    - Application 2:

    - Application 3:

- Assess your progress towards your goals and intentions.

    - Progress 1:

    - Progress 2:

    - Progress 3:

3. Challenges and Obstacles:

- Identify any challenges or obstacles you encountered this week and how you overcame them or plan to overcome them.

- Challenge 1:

- Challenge 2:

- Challenge 3:

4. Gratitude and Celebrations:

- List three things you are grateful for this week.

- Gratitude 1:

- Gratitude 2:

- Gratitude 3:

- Celebrate your achievements, successes, and positive experiences from this week.

- Celebration 1:

- Celebration 2:

- Celebration 3:

5. Next Week's Focus:

- Set your intentions and focus for the upcoming week.

    - Intention 1:

    - Intention 2:

    - Intention 3:

- Identify any areas for improvement or adjustments you can make in the coming week.

    - Improvement 1:

    - Improvement 2:

    - Improvement 3:

Take some time to review and complete this template at the end of each week to reflect on your progress, insights, and experiences.

This will help you stay on track with your goals, celebrate your successes, and continually grow and evolve on your Reality Transurfing journey.

Notes

Week 4:
Mastering Reality Transurfing and Moving Forward

Notes

Day.22
Creating a Supportive Environment

Book Insight

Creating a supportive environment and connecting with like-minded individuals enhances your Reality Transurfing journey.

Daily Challenge

Reflect on your current environment and the people in your life, and consider any changes you can make to create a more supportive atmosphere for your Reality Transurfing journey.

Affirmation

I surround myself with people and environments that uplift and support my growth.

Reflect on your current environment and the people in your life.

Write about any changes you can make to create a more supportive and uplifting environment for your Reality Transurfing journey.

Describe how you can connect with like-minded individuals who share your interest in Reality Transurfing.

Notes

Day.23
Overcoming Limiting Beliefs

Book Insight

Overcoming limiting beliefs is crucial for manifesting your desired reality and embracing your full potential.

Daily Challenge

Identify three limiting beliefs that may be holding you back, and write about the steps you can take to overcome them.

Affirmation

I release limiting beliefs and embrace empowering beliefs that support my success.

Identify at least three limiting beliefs that may be holding you back from manifesting your desired reality.

Write about the steps you can take to overcome these limiting beliefs and replace them with empowering beliefs.

Notes

Day.24

Cultivating Patience and Persistence

Book Insight

Cultivating patience and persistence helps you stay committed to your Reality Transurfing journey and manifest your desired reality.

Daily Challenge

Reflect on your progress so far, and identify any areas where you may need to practice patience and persistence.

Affirmation

I am patient and persistent, knowing that my desired reality is unfolding in perfect timing.

Reflect on your progress so far and write about any areas where you may need to practice patience and persistence.

Describe how you can cultivate these qualities to support your Reality Transurfing journey.

Notes

Day.25
Celebrating Your Wins

Book Insight

Celebrating your wins helps you maintain a positive mindset and attract the Wave of Fortune.

Daily Challenge

List five achievements, successes, or positive experiences related to your Reality Transurfing journey so far.

Affirmation

I acknowledge and celebrate my achievements and successes, knowing they bring more abundance into my life.

List at least five achievements, successes, or positive experiences related to your Reality Transurfing journey so far.

Reflect on how celebrating your wins can help you maintain a positive mindset and attract the Wave of Fortune.

Notes

Day.26
Living in the Present Moment

Book Insight

Living in the present moment allows you to fully engage with your Reality Transurfing practice and manifest your desired reality.

Daily Challenge

Practice being fully present and engaged in the present moment throughout the day.

Affirmation

I embrace the present moment, knowing it is the key to creating my desired reality.

Practice being fully present and engaged in the present moment throughout the day.

Write about your experience and any insights you gained.

Describe how living in the present moment can support your Reality Transurfing practice.

Notes

Day.27
Preparing for the Future

Book Insight

Preparing for the future involves setting intentions and goals, as well as continuing to apply Reality Transurfing principles.

Daily Challenge

Reflect on your progress during this 30-day guided journal, and set intentions and goals for the future.

Affirmation

I am excited and prepared for the future, knowing that my desired reality is within my reach.

Reflect on the progress you've made during this 30-day guided journal and write about your intentions and goals for the future.

Describe how you can continue to apply Reality Transurfing principles to create the reality you desire.

Notes

Day.28
Final Reflections and Gratitude

Book Insight

Expressing gratitude for your experiences and growth during your Reality Transurfing journey helps you stay aligned with your desired reality.

Daily Challenge

Review your journal entries from the past 30 days and express gratitude for the lessons learned and progress made.

Affirmation

I am grateful for my growth, experiences, and insights on my Reality Transurfing journey.

Review your journal entries from the past 30 days and write about the insights, growth, and experiences you've had during this journey.

Express gratitude for the lessons learned and the progress you've made, and set your intentions for moving forward with Reality Transurfing.

Day.29

Book Insight

Reviewing your progress and insights from the 30-Day Guided Journal helps you integrate the lessons and experiences from your Reality Transurfing journey.

Daily Challenge

Review your journal entries from the past 29 days and write down any key insights, lessons, or breakthroughs you experienced during this time.

Affirmation

I reflect on my journey with gratitude and wisdom, using my experiences to guide my future growth.

Notes

Notes

Notes

Day.30

Book Insight

Completing the 30-Day Guided Journal is just the beginning of your Reality Transurfing journey.

Continuing to apply the principles and practices will help you manifest your desired reality more effectively.

Daily Challenge

Set intentions for how you will continue to apply Reality Transurfing principles in your life, and identify any areas where you would like to deepen your practice or understanding.

Affirmation

I am committed to my Reality Transurfing journey, knowing that my desired reality is within my reach.

Weekly Review and Reflection Template

1. Key Insights and Learnings:

- Reflect on the key insights and learnings from this week's journal entries, activities, and experiences.

    - Insight 1:

    - Insight 2:

    - Insight 3:

2. Application and Progress:

- Consider how you have applied the key insights and learnings in your daily life this week.

    - Application 1:

    - Application 2:

    - Application 3:

- Assess your progress towards your goals and intentions.

    - Progress 1:

    - Progress 2:

    - Progress 3:

3. Challenges and Obstacles:

- Identify any challenges or obstacles you encountered this week and how you overcame them or plan to overcome them.

    - Challenge 1:

    - Challenge 2:

    - Challenge 3:

4. Gratitude and Celebrations:

- List three things you are grateful for this week.

    - Gratitude 1:

    - Gratitude 2:

    - Gratitude 3:

- Celebrate your achievements, successes, and positive experiences from this week.

    - Celebration 1:

    - Celebration 2:

    - Celebration 3:

5. Next Week's Focus:

- Set your intentions and focus for the upcoming week.

    - Intention 1:

    - Intention 2:

    - Intention 3:

- Identify any areas for improvement or adjustments you can make in the coming week.

    - Improvement 1:

    - Improvement 2:

    - Improvement 3:

Take some time to review and complete this template at the end of each week to reflect on your progress, insights, and experiences.

This will help you stay on track with your goals, celebrate your successes, and continually grow and evolve on your Reality Transurfing journey.

Notes

Made in the USA
Las Vegas, NV
24 December 2023

83497378R00127